A TASTE OF GRATITUDE

DELICIOUS DISHES & POSITIVE VIBES

Karen Tui Boyes

Published by Spectrum Education Limited
Lower Hutt, New Zealand
info@spectrumeducation.com

ISBN 978-0-9951314-9-1

Copyright © Spectrum Education 2024
© Karen Tui Boyes 2024

Designed and typeset by Spectrum Education, New Zealand

All rights reserved. No part of this publication may be reproduced, stored in a retrieval system, or transmitted in any form or by any means (electronic, mechanical, photocopying or otherwise), without the prior written permission of both the copyright owner and the publisher of this book.

Hello, beautiful soul! 🌿✨

Hello! I'm so excited you are reading this. Before you delight in the contents of this book, I want to be clear. I'm not a chef, not a nutritionist, not a dietitian. I'm a mid-fifties woman on a vibrant journey to embrace life with boundless energy and vitality. My passion? Living a full, fun and energetic life, to have energy to burn for my future grandchildren – if I ever get some!

I'm a lifelong learner, valuing my health, discipline, and freedom. I want to live to be 120 years! Why? Because there's a bucket list waiting and adventures to embark on, and most importantly, I want to transform education globally. I need to be fit, strong, energetic and vital to do that. I aspire to be the person others inquire about, wondering, "What's she up to now?" I'm aiming to continue to embark on adventures, enjoy life, and make a positive impact with the one precious life I have.

Aging, for me, is a choice—a personal science experiment. I observe, question, learn, try something, tweak variables, and repeat. What works for me might not be your solution, and that's the beauty of our uniqueness!

That's why you have "A Taste of Gratitude" in your hands. It's not just a recipe book; it's a collection born from my wellness journey. These are the recipes requested after the Gratitude Retreats I host – a culmination of healthful delights to nourish your body, mind, and spirit. Plus, intermingled with the best life hack to living a fantastic life: GRATITUDE!

Join me on this journey of flavours, health, and joy. Let's savour every bite on the path to radiant life. 🌿🌟

Rainbows and sunshine 🌈☀️

Karen

PS: All the food featured in this book has been personally prepared by me and the accompanying photos are authentic captures of both the process and the delicious results.

Contents

RECIPES :

- 5   Asparagus, Halloumi & Zucchini Salad
- 7   Broccoli Salad
- 9   Cauliflower Pizza
- 11   Curry Egg Salad
- 13   Edamame Salad with Ginger Dressing
- 15   Eggplant, Tomato & Zucchini Bake
- 17   Fresh Green Salad
- 19   Lemon Asparagus with Parmesan
- 21   Nutty Quinoa Salad
- 23   Roasted Orange Carrots
- 25   Simple Lettuce Salad
- 27   Spinach, Walnut, Parmesan & Pear Salad
- 29   Vegetable Stock
- 31   Zucchini, Hazelnut, Parmesan Salad
- 33   Chocolate Nut Slice
- 35   Christmas Bark
- 37   Fruit & Nut Chocolate

EXTRA BITS :

- 39   The Fresh Factor
- 41   Eat a Rainbow
- 42   Message from Karen
- 43   Karen's Protocols
- 45   BLE Breakfast Options
- 46   BLE Lunch Options
- 47   BLE Dinner Options
- 49   About the Author

> Living in a state of gratitude is the gateway to grace.
>
> *Arianna Huffington*

Asparagus, Halloumi & Zucchini Salad

INGREDIENTS:

- 1-2 bunches of asparaus
- 1-2 zucchini
- 1 cup cherry tomatoes
- 1 packet of halloumi cheese
- Fresh basil leaves

DRESSING:

- Freshly squeezed juice from an orange
- 2 tsp seeded mustard

Mix the orange juice and mustard in a small jar. Screw on lid firmly and shake well. Taste. If not sweet enough, add 1/4 tsp of honey.

TIP: When cooking halloumi cheese, line the frypan with baking paper. This stops the cheese sticking and makes clean up easier.

HOW TO MAKE:

1. Half fill a large saucepan with water and bring to the boil.
2. Snap the woody ends off the asparagus and add to water thick ends first. Cook until a knife cuts through the stalks easily and remove from heat. Strain and add asparagus to a bowl of iced water to cool quickly. This ensures the asparagus stays bright green.
3. Using a vegetable peeler, peel the zucchini in long strips and layer at the bottom of a serving plate.
4. Cut the tomatoes in half and add to serving plate.
5. Slice the halloumi and cook in a frypan lined with baking paper. Turn when brown.
6. Arrange the asparagus and halloumi on the plate and sprinkle with torn basil leaves. Serve with dressing drizzled over top.

Broccoli Salad

Broccoli Salad

INGREDIENTS:

- 1 head of broccoli
- 1/2 red onion
- 1/3 cup dried cranberries
- 1/2 cup almonds
- 1/2 cup pumpkin seeds (optional)
- 1 tsp paprika
- 1 Tbsp tamari soy sauce
- 1 Tbsp olive oil

DRESSING:

- 3 Tbsp olive oil
- Juice from 1 orange
- 1 Tbsp apple cider vinegar
- 2 tsp Dijon mustard
- 1 tsp honey or maple syrup

In a jar, add all dressing ingredients together. Screw the lid on firmly and shake well.

HOW TO MAKE:

1. Heat oven to 180°C. In a small bowl, add almonds, pumpkin seeds, tamari, olive oil and paprika. Stir well. Place almonds on a baking sheet and bake 10-14 mins until golden brown. Remove from oven and let cool for 5 mins. They will get crisper as they cool.

2. Chop broccoli florets into bite-size pieces. Half-fill a medium saucepan with water and bring to the boil. Add broccoli to boiling water for 1-2 minutes. Drain quickly and run under cold water to cool quickly. This keeps the broccoli bright green.

3. Thinly slice red onion and mix with cranberries. Coat with dressing.

4. Toss onion mix with the cold broccoli. Serve chilled.

TIP: Cook the nuts in an airfryer for 5-6 mins at 180°C.

A Taste of Gratitude

Gratitude is the closest thing to beauty manifested in an emotion.

Mindy Kaling

Cauliflower Pizza

INGREDIENTS :

- 1 large whole cauliflower
- 3-4 firm tomatoes
- 1-2 red capsicum
- Basil pesto
- Pine nuts
- Parmesan cheese or favourite cheese
- Fresh basil leaves
- Black pepper

HOW TO MAKE :

1. Heat oven to 200°C. Line a baking tray with baking paper.
2. Cut whole cauliflower in half and slice 1cm slices to create pizza bases.
3. Arrange cauliflower bases on a baking tray and place them in the oven for 5-10 mins while you prepare the rest of the ingredients.
4. Slice tomatoes thinly, dice capsicum, chop basil leaves and grate cheese.
5. Remove cauliflower from oven and spread pesto over the base. Arrange tomatoes, capsicum, basil, nuts and sprinkle cheese on top. Dust with black pepper.
6. Bake for 8-15 minutes, until cheese is bubbly brown. Serve with a green salad or green beans.

TIP: You can add anything you love on a pizza to this base: ham, bacon, chicken, mushrooms, pineapple... the list is endless.

"Focusing on one thing that you are grateful for increases the energy of gratitude and raises the joy inside yourself."

Oprah

Curry Egg Salad

INGREDIENTS:

- 4-8 hard boiled eggs
- 1/2 carrot
- 1/2 red onion
- 3 stalks celery
- 2 Tbsp fresh coriander
- 1/4 cup cashews
- 1/4 cup sultanas

DRESSING:

- Juice from 1/2 orange
- 1/4 cup olive oil
- 1 tsp curry powder
- 1/2 tsp ground turmeric
- 2 tsp lime juice
- 1/2 - 1 tsp honey to taste
- Salt and pepper to taste

HOW TO MAKE:

1. Shred or grate the carrot.
2. Dice the onion and chop the celery and corriander finely.
3. Dry roast the cashews for 5 minutes in an air fryer or for 5-8 minutes in the oven at 180ºC. Cool for 5 minutes.
4. Combine carrot, onion, celery, corriander, cashews and saltanas into a serving bowl or plate. Stir in dressing.
5. Shell the eggs, cut in half or quarters and add on top of the salad ingredients. Serve chilled.
This salad is often better the day after making it, as the dressing soaks in.

TO MAKE DRESSING:

Combine all ingredients in a bowl or jar and whisk or shake until smooth.

A Taste of Gratitude

Wear gratitude like a cloak, and it will feed every corner of your life.

Rumi

Edamame Salad with Ginger Dressing

SALAD INGREDIENTS :

- 2 cups shelled edamame beans
- 1/2 cup sliced red onion
- 1/2 cup diced cucumber
- 1 cup diced red capsicum
- 1/2 cup grated carrot
- 1/4 cup chopped coriander

DRESSING :

- 3 Tbsp tamari soy sauce
- 2 Tbsp fresh orane juice
- 1 Tbsp white wine vinegar
- 1 Tbsp olive oil
- 1 Tbsp honey
- 2 cloves garlic
- 1 Tbsp chopped ginger root

HOW TO MAKE :

1. Cook edamame in salted boiling water for 5-8 mins. Drain when cooked.
2. Combine all salad ingredients, drizzle with dressing and toss to combine. Chill and serve.

TO MAKE DRESSING :

3. Combine all ingredients in a blender and blend until smooth. Store in an airtight jar in the fridge.

"Enough" is a feast.
Buddhist Proverb

Eggplant, Tomato & Zucchini Bake

INGREDIENTS:

- 1 eggplant (aubergine)
- 1 large zucchini
- 2-3 firm tomatoes
- 1 red onion
- 1-2 tsp dried thyme
- 1/2 cup feta cheese

HOW TO MAKE:

1. Heat the oven to 200ºC.
2. Dice the red onion and place at bottom of heat proof dish. Sprinkle 1 tsp of thyme over onion.
3. Thinly slice eggplant, zucchini and tomatoes.
4. Arrange the sliced vegetables in the dish alternating the eggplant, zucchini and tomatoes, in a circle, until the dish is full.
5. Chop feta cheese and add between slices and scatter over top. Sprinkle remaining thyme over the top.
6. Bake, covered, in oven for 35-45 minutes until eggplant is cooked and cheese is golden brown.

Appreciation is a wonderful thing. It makes what is excellent in others belong to us as well.

Voltaire

Fresh Green Salad

INGREDIENTS:

- 2 cups mixed lettuce leaves
- 1/2 cucumber
- 1/2 cup snow pea sprouts
- 1/2 cup mung bean sprouts
- 1/4 cup fresh basil leaves
- 1 green apple
- 1 green pepper
- 1/2 cup snow peas
- 1 avacado
- 1/4 cup pumpkin seeds

DRESSING:

- 3 Tbsp olive oil
- 2 Tbsp red wine vinegar
- 1 tsp Dijon mustard
- 1 tsp honey or maple syrup

Add all dressing ingredients to a jar. Secure the lid and shake well.

HOW TO MAKE:

1. Toast the pumpkin seeds in the oven or airfryer at 180ºC for 5 minutes, stirring 3-4 times during cooking. Alternatively cook in a frypan over medium heat stirring contsantly. When golden brown, leave to cool.

2. Prepare the salad ingredients as follows:
   - Tear the lettuce leaves and add to the serving bowl.
   - Dice the cucumber and capsicum.
   - Chop the basil leaves.
   - Slice the apple thinly.
   - Cut the ends off the snow pea pods and chop into bite size pieces.
   - Halve the avocado, carefully cut into sections in the skin then use a spoon to scoop flesh out.

3. Add sprouts and all ingredients above into the serving bowl. Drizzle with dressing and toss well. Serve immediately.

A Taste of Gratitude

Lemon Asparagus with Parmesan

INGREDIENTS :

- 1-2 bunches asparagus
- 100g parmesan
- Juice of a lemon

TIP:
This recipe is great with the thicker spears of asparagus.
While cooking, test with a knife to determine whether the asparagus is cooked.

To stop the tips from over cooking, cover with a strip of baking paper or tin foil.

HOW TO MAKE :

1. Heat the oven to 200°C. Line a bake-proof dish or tray with nonstick baking paper.
2. Snap the woody ends off the asparagus and arrange on the paper.
3. Grate the cheese and sprinkle over the tops of the asparagus.
4. Drizzle olive oil and half the lemon juice over the asparagus.
5. Bake in the oven for 5-8 minutes, checking frequently. When tender, remove from oven, drizzle with remaining lemon juice and serve.

A Taste of Gratitude

Piglet noticed that even though he had a very small heart, it could hold a rather large amount of gratitude.

A.A. Milne
'Winnie-the-Pooh'

Nutty Quinoa Salad

INGREDIENTS:

- 1 cup quinoa
- 1 cup hazelnuts
- 2 medium beetroot
- 1/2 cup fresh coriander
- 2 oranges
- 1/4 cup fresh mint leaves

DRESSING:

- 1/4 cup olive oil
- 2 Tbsp fresh orange juice
- 2 Tbsp balsamic vinegar
- 1 tsp honey
- Salt and pepper to taste

TO MAKE DRESSING:

Combine all ingredients in a bowl or jar and whisk or shake until smooth.

HOW TO MAKE:

1. Cook quinoa in simmering water for 10-15 minutes. Drain and let cool.

2. Peel and dice beetroot. Roast in a 175°C oven for 30-40 mins or until tender. At same time, roast hazelnuts in a 175°C oven for 10-12 mins until skins start to crack. Let cool and rub them between a clean tea towel to remove the skins. Chop hazelnuts roughly.

3. Peel the oranges and chop into small bite size pieces. Chop the coriander and mint.

4. Combine all salad ingredients, drizzle with dressing and toss to combine. Chill and serve.

A Taste of Gratitude

> When we focus on our gratitude, the tide of disappointment goes out and the tide of love rushes in.
>
> *Kristin Armstrong*

Roasted Orange Carrots

INGREDIENTS :

- 4-5 carrots
- 1 orange
- Olive oil
- 1 tsp sesame seeds

HOW TO MAKE :

1. Heat oven to 200ºC and line a baking tray of dish with baking paper.
2. Peel carrots, remove ends and cut into long strips.
3. Arrange carrot sticks in a single layer on a baking tray or dish.
4. Juice the orange and pour 1/2 of the juice over the carrots. Lightly drizzle the carrots with olive oil.
5. Roast for 20 - 30 minutes turning the carrots over half way through cooking.
6. When cooked, arrange on a serving plate. Top with remaining orange juice and dust with sesame seeds.

Simple Lettuce Salad

Simple Lettuce Salad

INGREDIENTS :

- Lettuce leaves - mixed varieties or your favourite
- Cucumber
- Snow peas
- Red capsicums
- Pumpkin seeds
- Hard boiled eggs
- Cherry tomatoes
- Ripe avocado

DRESSING :

Use your favourite dressing.

TIP: Add fresh basil, toasted sunflower seeds, mushrooms or grated carrot.

HOW TO MAKE :

1. Roast the pumpkin seeds in air fryer, frypan or in oven. Set aside to cool.
2. Rip or chop the lettuce and cover the bottom of a serving bowl or plate.
3. Dice the cucumber and capsicum and layer on top of lettuce.
4. Cut the ends off the snowpeas and cut into 1 cm bite-size pieces. Add to bowl or plate.
5. Shell the eggs, cut in half and halve the cherry tomatoes. Arrange on top of salad.
6. Halve avocado, remove stone, score the flesh gently with a knife. Use a spoon to scoop out and add to salad.
7. Sprinkle with cooled pumpkin seeds and toss gently to mix. Serve chilled.

When eating fruit, remember the one who planted the tree.

Vietnamese Proverb

Spinach, Walnut, Parmesan & Pear Salad

INGREDIENTS:

- 1-2 cups baby spinach leaves
- 3/4 cup walnuts
- 1-2 pears
- 100g parmesan cheese

DRESSING:

- 1 cup balsamic vinegar
- 1 tsp honey

In a small saucepan, mix the vinegar and honey. Bring to the boil over a high heat then reduce the heat and simmer for 5-8 minutes. Keep a close watch and stir often to avoid burning. The liquid will reduce by half and is ready when it thickens and sticks to the back of a spoon. Cool. Store in an airtight jar in fridge.

HOW TO MAKE:

1. Roast the walnuts in the oven at 175°C for 10-12 minutes. Stir halfway through cooking. Cool when golden in colour.
2. Arrange spinach leaves on serving plate.
3. Using a vegetable peeler, or the slicing side of a grater, slice parmersan cheese into thin slices.
4. Quarter, core and thinly slice the pears.
5. Arrange the walnuts, parmesan and pear on top of the spinach. Drizzle with dressing and serve immediately.

TIP: I use parmesan because it is low fat and easy to digest, however replace with blue cheese in this recipe if you desire.

> **Acknowledging the good that you already have in your life is the foundation for all abundance.**
>
> *Eckhart Tolle*

Vegetable Stock

INGREDIENTS:

- Broccoli leaves and stalks
- Cauliflower leaves and stalks
- 1 white onion
- Celery stalks and leaves
- 1-2 carrots
- 1 Tbsp black pepper corns
- 5-6 bay leaves
- 4-5 cups of water

HOW TO MAKE:

1. Chop all the vegetables, stems, stalks and leaves to 2-3 cm bits. Add to the largest saucepan you have.
2. Add water, peppercorns and bay leaves.
3. Bring to the boil and simmer with lid on for 15-20 minutes.
4. Turn heat off and leave to cool.
5. Strain and freeze the liquid in containers. When required, add frozen stock directly to soups and casseroles.

TIP: After we have been to the weekly vegetable market, we use many of the stalks to make this beautiful stock.

TIP: Once the liquid has been strained off, you can use the hand blender, whizz or NutriBullet to mince the remaining veges and freeze the pulp in icecube trays. To use, add 3-4 cubes to your soups and casseroles with 1-2 cups of water.

TIP: Other vegetables, peelings or ends you could add include:
- parsnip
- swede
- kumera
- leeks
- mushrooms

A Taste of Gratitude

> It is not happiness that makes us grateful.
> It's gratefulness that makes us happy.
>
> *David Steindl-Rast*

Zucchini, Hazelnut, Parmesan Salad

INGREDIENTS:

- 3-4 zucchinis
- 1/2 cup hazelnuts
- 80g parmesan
- Basil leaves
- Balsamic vinegar

TIP: Use baking paper on the sandwich press, top and bottom, to make clean up fast!

HOW TO MAKE:

1. Roast hazelnuts in oven at 200°C for 10-12 mins or in an airfryer for 5 mins. Watch and stir to prevent burning. When cooked, allow to cool and rub the nuts between two tea towels to remove the skins. Chop roughly.
2. Chop the ends off the zucchinis and slice in half lengthwise.
3. Grill zucchini on sandwich press or BBQ until charred and still firm. Cut into 2-3 cm pieces.
4. Grate the cheese and chop or tear the basil leaves.
5. Combine zucchini, nuts, parmesan, and basil on a serving plate. Drizzle with balsamic vinegar and serve warm.

A Taste of Gratitude

> In the modern world, we are surrounded by so much abundance that we cannot see it.
>
> *Chris Matakas*

Chocolate Nut Slice

INGREDIENTS :

- 1 cup walnuts
- 1 cup almonds
- 3/4 cup of dates
- 1 cup rolled oats
- 2 Tbsp cacao or cocoa powder
- 3 Tbsp tahini (sesame butter)

ICING :

- 100g dark chocolate
- 1 Tbsp coconut oil
- A handful of chopped walnuts

HOW TO MAKE :

1. Mix the nuts and dates in a heat-proof bowl and cover with boiling water. Soak for 30 mins and strain, retaining 1/4 cup of the water.

2. Blend the nuts and dates in a food processor until roughly chopped.

3. Add oats, cacao or cocoa powder and tahini. Blend until combined. You will need to blend for 1 minute, scrape down the sides and repeat several times. If the mixture needs more moisture, add 1-2 Tbsps of retained liquid. Mixture should hold together when squeezed.

4. Press into a lined slice tin and chill in the fridge.

5. Melt the chocolate and coconut oil in a bowl in the microwave, or over very low heat, in a saucepan on the stovetop. Stir often to ensure it doesn't burn.

6. Spread over the base, sprinkle with walnuts and refrigerate until set. Slice with a warm knife and store in the fridge or freezer.

This recipe has been inspired and modified from Lauren Parson's Choc Nut Bliss Slice.

What separates privilege from entitlement is gratitude.

Brené Brown

Christmas Bark

INGREDIENTS:

- 1/2 block dark chocolate
- 1/2 block white chocolate
- 2 tsp coconut oil
- 3-4 candy canes
- a handful of green & red smarties or pebbles

TIP: I use Whittakers chocolate - it's a little more expensive - and worth it!!

HOW TO MAKE:

1. Line a baking tray or tin with baking paper.
2. Carefully melt each chocolate with 1 tsp of coconut oil in separate bowls in the microwave or over a very low heat, in two saucepans on the stovetop. Stir often to ensure it doesn't burn.
3. Using a big spoon, drop blobs of chocolate on the tray, alternating between brown and white, allowing the blobs to touch. Use a fork to lightly swirl the chocolate together.
4. Break up candy canes and sprinkle on top of chocolate. Dot pebbles on top.
5. Leave in the fridge until set. Break up with a knife and serve. Create beautiful gifts in cellophane or paper bags with ribbons. Store in the fridge or freezer.

A Taste of Gratitude

> Gratitude is a powerful catalyst for happiness. It's the spark that lights a fire of joy in your soul.
>
> *Amy Collette*

Fruit & Nut Chocolate

INGREDIENTS :

- 1 cup of your favourite nuts, roasted or plain
- 1 cup salty prezels
- 1 firm banana
- 1/2 cup frozen blueberries
- 1/2 cup shredded coconut
- 1 block of dark chocolate
- 2 tsp coconut oil

HOW TO MAKE :

1. Line a baking tray or tin with baking paper.
2. Cut the banana in half lengthwise and cut into thin slices. Roast nuts if desired.
3. Carefully melt the chocolate with the coconut oil, either in a bowl in the microwave or over very low heat, in a saucepan on the stovetop. Stir often to ensure it doesn't burn.
4. Arrange all ingredients on the tray and pour over the melted chocolate.
5. Leave in the fridge until set. Break up with a knife and serve.
Create beautiful gifts in cellophane or paper bags with ribbons. Store in the fridge or freezer.

> When I started counting my blessings, my whole life turned around.
>
> *Willie Nelson*

The Fresh Factor

One of the easiest ways to eat well is to have fresh fruit and vegetables available and displayed beautifully. Visit the local vegetable market each week and select the best and freshest food to eat throughout the week. If you don't have a farmers market, select the best from your supermarket.

Ultimately, being able to grow your own and select from your garden would be divine - plus food always tastes better when homegrown. Consider cultivating a small vegetable patch or growing vegetables in pots if you can. Growing herbs on your window sill is a great way to add freshness to your daily cooking.

Displaying the food, means you are more likely to think about it and reach for a healthier option if it is readily available. The bright colours make the food even more appealing.

Tomatoes taste better when left out of the fridge and avocados will ripen in a fruit bowl or on the bench. Once an avocado is ripe, store it in the fridge. When bananas are at your favourite ripeness, pop them in the fridge and they will stay fresh and stop ripening. The skins may go brown in the fridge, however the banana will be just as you like it on the inside.

> Always be thankful for what you have, because you never know when it might be gone.
>
> — Micalea Smeltzer

Eat a Rainbow

The 'Eat a Rainbow' approach encourages eating a wide variety of fruits and vegetables with each colour representing a special mix of nutrients and health benefits. As you check out the vibrant colours in the produce section, imagine not just a regular meal but a visually appealing and nutritious plate that turns ordinary eating into a feast for your eyes and body. Here's a breakdown of some of the benefits that come with adding fruits and veggies of different colours to your plate.

- **Red:** Red fruits and vegetables, such as tomatoes, strawberries, and red peppers, often contain antioxidants like lycopene and anthocyanins. These compounds are linked to heart health and reduced inflammation and may even have cancer-fighting properties.

- **Orange:** These colours signal the presence of beta-carotene, which the body converts into vitamin A. Carrots, sweet potatoes, oranges, and mangoes fall into this category, contributing to eye health, immune function, and skin integrity.

- **Yellow:** Yellow foods such as bananas, pineapples, and yellow bell peppers, are rich in vitamin C, support immune function, promote skin health, and act as potent antioxidants. Yellow foods like turmeric contribute anti-inflammatory properties, while those containing lutein and zeaxanthin, such as corn and yellow peppers, aid in maintaining eye health.

- **Green:** Leafy greens like spinach and kale, as well as broccoli and green apples, are rich in chlorophyll, vitamins, and minerals. They support bone health, promote digestion, and offer a host of antioxidants.

- **Blue and Purple:** Blueberries, grapes, and eggplants owe their rich colour to anthocyanins, which have been associated with improved cognitive function, cardiovascular health, and anti-aging properties.

- **White and Brown:** While not as colourful, foods like cauliflower, onions, garlic, and mushrooms offer essential nutrients. They often contain allicin, quercetin, and other compounds associated with immune support and anti-inflammatory effects.

Message from Karen

My health is a top value for me and conscientiously monitoring my dietary choices is a key strategy in sustaining optimal energy and vitality. I hold my body in high regard, viewing it as a temple that houses my soul, purpose and reason for existence on this planet. I think of food as the essential fuel for my remarkable body. Like caring for a car, the type and quantity of fuel you use significantly impacts performance. Taking charge of what enters my body is a personal responsibility, and I can testify that with a commitment to clean eating, my thinking is sharp and responsive and I have high energy.

While some might label me as obsessive about my health, I embrace this characteristic wholeheartedly. A common inquiry I receive, especially after an 8-hour day of presentations or facilitation, is, "How do you maintain such high energy levels?" The truth is (and most people don't really want to know the answer!) that the answer involves discipline, time investment, and consistent focus. It's not an effortless journey, but the rewards are undoubtedly worth the effort.

Years of dedicated research, learning, and proactive measures have led me to identify what works uniquely for me. Recognising the individuality of each person, there's no one-size-fits-all solution. Personally, I have had a vegetarian lifestyle for over 25 years, as it aligns with my sense of well-being, providing me with heightened energy levels. The principles I follow are fundamental, yet adaptable to personal needs. Please do your own inquiries and action research to see what works best for you.

On the next pages, you will find an outline of my eating plan inspired by Bright Line Eating plus the daily protocols and agreements I have with myself. Please be aware this eating plan is designed for a woman in her fifties.

Self-care is something you do every day - not just at the weekends or holidays. Start with one thing! Personally, I add, or subtract one thing each month - that is 12 new habits a year. Take it slow. I'm far from perfect and am working on my personal mastery every day. It is a journey and you are worth it!

Rainbows and sunshine *Karen*

Karen's Protocols

1st drink of the day:
Hot water, fresh lemon juice & 5 thin slices of ginger root. Boosts the immune system, enhances digestive and gut health

3 meals per day:
Balanced meals with protein, carbohydrates, and healthy fat

No snacking:
Eat substantial and nutritious meals to prevent hunger, thereby being able to refrain from indulging in snacks between meals

Stay hydrated:
Drink water, no tea, no coffee, no juice, no alcohol. Only water; hot, warm or room temp - in a pretty glass.
"Drink more water 'til you've got clear wees!"

Intermittent fasting:
Stop eating at 7pm and fast for at least 13 hours - everyday. This gives the digestive system time to work, rest and boosts energy

Starchy Carbs:
Minimise all bread, potatoes, rice, white flour and processed sugar

Daily body conditioning:
Move everyday: <u>stretch</u> to activate and wake up the muscles, to maintain flexibility & balance, <u>lift</u> heavy things to build muscle and do something to <u>increase the heart rate</u>

Practice Gratitude:
Each day find and record at least 3 things to be grateful for. Practice on the easy days so it is easier on the hard days

I am worthy:
Approach each meal with the mindset of hosting a valued guest for dinner and diligently prepare the best nutritious recipes every day. I'm worth it! You are worth it!

A Taste of Gratitude

> **By practising gratitude, we can actually wire our brains to help us build resilience.**
>
> *— Christina Costa*

BREAKFAST
For a healthier you

YOU are capable of AMAZING things!

1 X PROTEIN

CHOOSE ONE:
- 2 x eggs
- 50g cheese
- 100g ricotta cheese
- 50g nuts or nut butter
- 50g seeds
- 225g plain yoghurt
- 225g milk: dairy/soy/almond/hemp/rice

1 X BREAKFAST GRAIN

CHOOSE ONE:
- 25g rolled oats/oatmeal
- 100g quinoa
- 100g millet
- 100g sweet potato
- 100g brown rice

175G X FRUIT

CHOOSE FROM:
apple, pear, orange, banana, grapefruit, peach, nectarine, plum, kiwi, cherries, apricot, berries, grapes, pineapple, melon, mango.

This is the Female Intake Chart. Adapted from Bright Line Eating by Susan Peirce Thompson

LUNCH
For a healthier you

Because you are worth it!

1 X PROTEIN

1

CHOOSE ONE:
- 2 x eggs
- 50g cheese
- 100g cottage/ricotta cheese
- 50g nuts or nut butter
- 50g seeds
- 100g tofu/chicken/pork/beef/fish
- 100g edamame beans

175G VEGETABLES

2

asparagus, beetroot, brussel sprouts, broccoli, cabbage, carrots, celery, cucumber, eggplant, green beans, kale, lettuce, leeks, mushroom, onion, peppers, snow peas, spinach, tomatoes

175G X FRUIT

3

CHOOSE FROM:
apple, pear, orange, banana, gratefruit, peach, nectarine, plum, kiwi, cherries, apricot, berries, grapes, pineapple, melon, mango.

1 X FAT

4

CHOOSE FROM:
- 50g avocado
- 15g seeds/tahini
- 1 Tablespoon butter/nut butter/oil/mayonnaise

This is the Female Intake Chart. Adapted from Bright Line Eating by Susan Peirce Thompson

DINNER

For a healthier you

Stay STRONG and true to yourself!

1 X PROTEIN

CHOOSE ONE:
- 2 x eggs
- 50g cheese
- 100g cottage/ricotta cheese
- 50g nuts or nut butter
- 50g seeds
- 100g tofu/chicken/pork/beef/fish
- 100g edamame beans

175G VEGETABLES

asparagus, beetroot, brussels sprouts, broccoli, cabbage, carrots, cauliflower celery, cucumber, eggplant, green beans, kale, lettuce, leeks, mushroom, onion, peppers, snow peas, spinach, tomatoes

225G X SALAD

MAKE A SALAD WITH:
lettuce, spinach, tomatoes, cucumber, red onion, celery, carrots, peppers, beetroot, mushroom (or any of the vegetables above)

1 X FAT

CHOOSE FROM:
- 50g avocado
- 1 Tablespoon butter/nut butter/oil/mayonnaise
- 15g seeds/tahini

This is the Female Intake Chart. Adapted from Bright Line Eating by Susan Peirce Thompson